"Christians are pressed by very real questions. How does Scripture structure a church, order worship, organize ministry, and define biblical leadership? Those are just examples of the questions that are answered clearly, carefully, and winsomely in this new series from 9Marks. I am so thankful for this ministry and for its incredibly healthy and hopeful influence in so many faithful churches. I eagerly commend this series."

R. Albert Mohler Jr., President, The Southern Baptist Theological Seminary

"Sincere questions deserve thoughtful answers. If you're not sure where to start in answering these questions, let this series serve as a diving board into the pool. These minibooks are winsomely to-the-point and great to read together with one friend or one hundred friends."

Gloria Furman, author, *Missional Motherhood* and *The Pastor's Wife*

"As a pastor, I get asked lots of questions. I'm approached by unbelievers seeking to understand the gospel, new believers unsure about next steps, and maturing believers wanting help answering questions from their Christian family, friends, neighbors, or coworkers. It's in these moments that I wish I had a book to give them that was brief, answered their questions, and pointed them in the right direction for further study. Church Questions is a series that provides just that. Each booklet tackles one question in a biblical, brief, and practical manner. The series may be called Church Questions, but it could be called 'Church Answers.' I intend to pick these up by the dozens and give them away regularly. You should too."

Juan R. Sanchez, Senior Pastor, High Pointe Baptist Church, Austin, Texas

"Where can we Christians find reliable answers to our common questions about life together at church—without having to plow through long, expensive books? The Church Questions booklets meet our need with answers that are biblical, thoughtful, and practical. For pastors, this series will prove a trustworthy resource for guiding church members toward deeper wisdom and stronger unity."

Ray Ortlund, President, Renewal Ministries

Why Should I Give to My Church?

Church Questions

Why Should I Give to My Church?

Jamie Dunlop

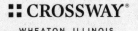

CROSSWAY®

WHEATON, ILLINOIS

Trade paperback ISBN: 978-1-4335-7243-2
ePub ISBN: 978-1-4335-7246-3
PDF ISBN: 978-1-4335-7244-9
Mobipocket ISBN: 978-1-4335-7245-6

Library of Congress Cataloging-in-Publication Data

Names: Dunlop, Jamie, author.
Title: Why should I give to my church? / Jamie Dunlop.
Description: Wheaton, Illinois : Crossway, [2021] | Series: Church questions | Includes bibliographical references and index.
Identifiers: LCCN 2020028969 (print) | LCCN 2020028970 (ebook) | ISBN 9781433572432 (trade paperback) | ISBN 9781433572449 (pdf) | ISBN 9781433572456 (mobi) | ISBN 9781433572463 (epub)
Subjects: LCSH: Christian giving.
Classification: LCC BV772 .D86 2021 (print) | LCC BV772 (ebook) | DDC 254/.8—dc23
LC record available at https://lccn.loc.gov/2020028969
LC ebook record available at https://lccn.loc.gov/2020028970

Crossway is a publishing ministry of Good News Publishers.

BP		31	30	29	28	27	26	25	24	23	22	21
14	13	12	11	10	9	8	7	6	5	4	3	2

Each one must give as he has decided in his heart, not reluctantly or under compulsion, for God loves a cheerful giver. And God is able to make all grace abound to you, so that having all sufficiency in all things at all times, you may abound in every good work.

2 Corinthians 9:7–8

**God Doesn't Need Your Money
(But He Cares That You Give)**

The Question: Why Give?

Why should you give to your church? It's an important question for two reasons. First, while giving seems as popular as ever in society, giving to a *church* is falling out of style. In the United States, at least, the portion of charitable giving going to churches dropped from 53 percent to 32 percent over the last thirty years.[1] The average Christian today gives 2.5 percent of their income to their church, versus 3.3 percent during the Great Depression.[2]

But second, it's an important question because the Bible's answer is quite different from what we might expect. Answering this "why" question is critical if we're going to answer other questions about giving, like how much you should give, to whom you should give, and how you should give.

Most of this book will focus on answering the "why" question. Then, with that foundation laid, we'll ask what role your church should play in your giving. Finally, we'll get to some more specific questions you might have.

The Bible: A Radically Different Perspective

To answer this "why" question, we must see how different the Bible's motivation for giving is from why most people give to charitable causes. Why do people generally give? Two words come to mind: need and obligation.

- Need: we give because good things need to get done—like relief after a natural disaster or sharing the gospel in an unreached city.
- Obligation: we give because we're supposed to. It's the right response to how much we've been blessed.

Yet the New Testament presents different motivations for giving. Two quick examples.

First, 1 Corinthians 13:3 tells us that "if I give away all I have . . . but have not love, I gain nothing." Fascinating! In God's eyes, the value of the gift comes not from how badly it's needed, but from whether or not I give in *love*. Give for the wrong reasons and what you've done is of no value at all, no matter the worthiness of the need you're meeting.

Second, we read in 2 Corinthians 9:7 that "God loves a cheerful giver." Really? Does the Red Cross care about your motives when you write a check? Do politicians care about *why* you're supporting their campaigns? Yet it is the *cheerful* giver who pleases God. That's quite contrary to giving because you have to.

Obligation and need don't factor very prominently in the New Testament's teaching about giving.[3] Instead, we see things like opportunity and joy, God's glory and reward. Why is this?

The Problem with Obligation

Let me give you an illustration. My wife is an excellent cook. Of course, my three school-aged kids don't always see it that way. At times, they complain. So picture this: on one day, they eat ravenously, raving about how good dinner is. The next day, they aren't fans of the food, but they eat it anyway without complaining. Which day shows off my wife's culinary skills? The first, of course. Day two merely extols my kids and their obedience.

In the same way, giving out of obligation shows off how obedient *we* are. But giving with joy (or with "cheer" [2 Cor. 9:7]) glorifies God.[4] When we gladly part with our money in order to follow Christ, it proclaims how good and worthy he is.

Remember that God in no way *needs* our giving. In Psalm 50:12, God says "If I were hungry, I would not tell you, for the world and its fullness are mine." *Everything* belongs to God. Even the money we think we're "giving to him" already belongs to him. God has never once been frustrated for lack of money.

So why does God care about our giving? Not because he needs our money, but because he wants our hearts. That's why God wants a cheerful giver.

Joyful Giving

I remember meeting Jeff Bezos the year after he started Amazon. If you're reading this in a different part of the world, think of meeting Jack Ma of Alibaba or Marcos Galperin of MercadoLibre. At the time, he was a nobody with a big idea. Now, let's imagine (sadly, this is only in our imaginations) he asked me for a few thousand dollars in exchange for a piece of the company. Looking back, I wouldn't see that exchange as doing *him* a favor, would I? By now, that stake would be worth millions of dollars. I'd consider it one of the greatest, most spectacular opportunities I'd ever encountered!

That is the attitude God calls you to have as you give to your church. That excitement, that joy, that anticipation—and beyond—are foundational to giving well. We should strive to see giving as opportunity, not obligation. Not in the way some religious hucksters tell us to give on TV that distorts and profanes God's promises in Scripture, those who say "give to my ministry and God will make you wealthy." No, we give to gain something much, much better—both in this world and the world to come.

To see that, we'll spend the next three sections asking the question, *Why should we give?* These sections will be much more useful if you can compare them with your honest answers to the same question. So in the spaces below, take a moment (without peeking ahead!) and write down the three main reasons you give to your church. Yes—for real—take a moment to do this; it'll make the next three sections much more useful for you.

Why I give to my church:

1. _____

   _____

2. _____

   _____

3. _____

   _____

Why Give? For Your Heart

When Money Flies Away

I once took a business trip to London in the years before I became a pastor. My last night there, I decided to call into a church meeting back home—and it turned out to be a long, six-hour meeting. The next morning, two things happened that I'll never forget. First, I learned I was getting a sizable bonus from my employer, which immediately got me thinking how I would spend it. How much should I spend? How much should I give? And the more I thought of ways to spend it, the smaller the portion I intended to give away grew.

Second, as I was checking out of my hotel, I learned that the toll-free number I'd dialed into for the long church meeting wasn't actually toll-free, and I was being charged £10 per minute for my phone call. Do the math . . . that's thousands of dollars! Who knew the Lord had such a sense of humor? He'd given me a sizable chunk of money, I'd immediately thought about how to spend it on myself, and then he'd taken it away.

What a wonderful illustration of how Proverbs 23:4–5 describes the fleeting nature of wealth.

> Do not toil to acquire wealth;
>> be discerning enough to desist.

When your eyes light on it, it is gone,
> for suddenly it sprouts wings,
> flying like an eagle toward heaven.

Don't give your heart to something like that!
As it turns out, losing that money was good for my heart! Suddenly I realized the trap I'd fallen into with the "good fortune" of my bonus.

Thankfully, I was able to negotiate with the hotel manager and got my phone bill reduced to just a few dollars. I gave the bonus to my church and a missionary. I needed God's reminder that this money belonged to God, and that my stewardship of it could be quite fleeting. That understanding released the money's stranglehold on my heart, and it was a joy to be generous.

Our Hearts Follow Our Treasure

That's just what Jesus told us, isn't it? "Lay up for yourselves treasures in heaven. . . . For where your treasure is, there your heart will be also" (Matt. 6:20–21). Our hearts naturally follow our treasure. If you buy stock in Nike, you'll have a sudden interest in how Nike is doing. If you give—and live—such that most of your treasure is waiting for you in heaven, that's where your heart will be.

Laying up treasure in heaven is one of the Bible's main arguments for why we should give: it protects our hearts from becoming attached to the things of this world.

In fact, this connection between hearts and treasure works in two directions. Your heart will *follow* your treasure. But in addition, the condition of your heart *reveals* your treasure. If you're a Christian, you should be living so that if heaven turns out not to be real, your life will have been an utter failure, a calamity (1 Cor. 15:19). Your calling is to put all your eggs in one basket: the basket of Jesus's promises. And you'll know how well you're doing that by looking at your heart.

How much do you long for heaven, and how much do you long for the enticements of *this* world? That's Matthew 6 as a thermometer, taking the temperature of your life.

But what if you discover that your heart is overly consumed with the things of this world? Give those things away. Put your treasure in heaven, and your heart will follow. That's

Matthew 6 as a thermostat, *adjusting* the temperature of your affections.

What Does Your Giving Say about Your Heart?

God asks you to give because he wants your heart. He wants your desires and dreams and affections and ambitions to be built on *him* and *his* promises, not on the things of this world that will surely disappoint and disappear. Do you see how kind and loving that is?

So take a moment to ask yourself these questions. Consider writing down your answers in the space provided:

What do you tend to daydream about?

What fears crowd in when you're alone?

What kind of goals do you set for yourself?

What mistakes do you most regret?

What do you most often talk about?

And what do these descriptors of your heart tell you about where your treasure really is?

God's Amazing Love

It's astounding, isn't it, that God cares about all this? The God who created and sustains the universe, the one who rules continents, planets, star systems, galaxies, time, and eternity—this God cares about what *you* do, and beyond that, *why* you do it. And he cares about what you do because he loves you. He is jealous for your joy.

So be generous with what God has entrusted to you—you need to, for the sake of your heart.

Why Give? For Your Reward

Paul's Strange Thank-You Note

The book of Philippians is, in part, a thank-you note from Paul to the church at Philippi for their financial support. Of course, thank-you notes are a great way to ask people to keep giving, which makes Paul's words at the end of Philippians rather unexpected.

> *Not* that I am speaking of being in need, for I have learned in whatever situation I am to be content. . . . I can do *all things* through him who strengthens me. (Phil. 4:11, 13)

Paul emphasizes that he *has no needs!* And yet, he was still thankful that they gave, not for his sake but for theirs.

> Not that I seek the gift, but I seek the fruit that increases to your credit. (Phil. 4:17)

He wants them to give because *they* get something out of giving. As Jesus said in Matthew 6, some things we do in this life will result in heavenly treasure. That's the second major reason the Bible gives for why you should give: eternal reward. In fact, if this doesn't factor into your decisions about money, your financial strategy is woefully short-sighted.

Sadly, because the so-called prosperity gospel has wreaked such havoc on Christian churches around the world, I should pause for a moment to emphasize that the reward Scripture promises is very real and is *spiritual* in nature. As Jesus says in Matthew 6, "Lay up for yourselves treasures *in heaven*" (v. 20). If you give more to your church, God *may* choose to increase your net worth today. But he has in no way promised such a thing. Any Christian teacher who promises—or insinuates—a better marriage, a better bank balance, or a better doctor's visit because you give to his or her ministry is no Christian teacher.[5]

Trade What's Disappearing for What Will Last

A few years ago, the government of India declared all five-hundred and one-thousand rupee banknotes to be null and void—effective *four hours* from the time of the announcement.

That'd be the equivalent of being told that all ten and twenty dollar bills in your wallet will be of no use starting sometime this afternoon. What would you do with those soon-to-be-worthless bills? You'd likely turn them in for a currency that will last, wouldn't you?

What a magnificent illustration of the Christian life! You can't take it with you. But, as many have said, you *can* send it on ahead. Just like those merchants in India busily exchanging soon-to-be-worthless currency, you can exchange worldly wealth for treasure that will last by giving it away to fuel gospel work. What you do with your money *today* will impact you *forever*.

Be Deliberate with Your Money

This reality calls for a careful approach to money. But sadly, such an approach doesn't describe all of us. Some of us are not deliberate with our money because we don't have much. But consider the heroes of giving in the Bible: freed Egyptian slaves giving to the tabernacle (Exodus 36); Macedonian Christians giving out of extreme poverty (2 Corinthians 8); the poor widow of Mark 12 giving all that she had to live on—and receiving praise from the Son of God. The giving heroes of the Bible were *poor*! It's interesting, in 1 Timothy 6, when Paul addresses the wealthy, he tells them to "do good, to be *rich in good works*, . . . and ready to share" (v. 18). An economist might say the generosity of the poor doesn't matter much because their gifts are small. But in God's economy, it's precisely the opposite. The *poor* are the giving heroes of the Bible. The rich are expected to be generous—but what God *really* wants from them is to be rich in good deeds. Gifts out of scarcity are what most honor God.

On the other hand, for some of us a failure to be deliberate with our money actually feels virtuous. *Yeah . . . I'm just not really into money. You can't take it with you, right?* To the contrary, the financially ambivalent must remember that how we view money is a key indicator of faith. In Jesus's famous parable of the talents in Matthew 25, the master called the servant who was ambivalent about stewarding his wealth "wicked and slothful" (v. 26), and his end is a warning to us all.

You should give, not only because it's good for your heart, but because by giving you are laying up for yourself treasure in heaven that will never be destroyed.

Why Give? For God's Glory

How Giving Glorifies God

A third reason to give is that giving shows off the goodness and glory of God. How? To borrow an analogy from John Piper: Why do I give my wife flowers? Not because I have to (imagine the look on her face if that's what I told her) but because I *want* to. Because she's amazing! Because she's delightful! Because I want, in some small way, to communicate all my feelings of love for and delight in her to her.[6]

In the same way, our hearts will swell with a desire to give when they swell with an appreciation for how amazing God is. He is the one who created all things. The goodness we enjoy in clear mountain air, in a sweet friendship, in a job well done, in a delicious meal is *his* goodness. And those things are merely the faintest shadows of how good he really is. His goodness, in fact, extends far beyond simply creating the world—he will also one day judge the world. He is so good that there is not one false deed that will not be exposed, not one wrong that will not be found out. One day, his righteousness will be so clear that "all nations will come and worship" him (Rev. 15:4).

Even more, our God is overflowing with the goodness of mercy. While we were dead in our sins, God "made us alive together with Christ" (Eph. 2:5). While we were his enemies, God sent his precious Son to die in our place (Rom. 5:8–10). Then, having done that, he has showered blessing upon blessing on us! The blessing of adoption as his sons and daughters. The blessing of his Spirit in us, who is a guarantee of the blessing of life forever with our Savior. The blessing of knowing that he is turning all things to our good (Rom. 8:28). The blessing of prayer, of God's perfect Word, of Christian love, of heaven. And I could go on!

How do we respond to the incalculable wealth of the goodness of God? We proclaim it! We proclaim it as we talk about it with our

Christian brothers and sisters. We proclaim it as we share the good news of Jesus with those who don't know him. And we proclaim it as we give our money away to make these things possible because Jesus is so much better. This is how our giving shows off the goodness and glory of God. Or, to use a more biblical term, this is how our money *glorifies* him. The family that gladly throws a million-dollar wedding for their daughter shows off their love for her and the extravagance of their wealth. The Christian who gladly gives of her material wealth shows off her love for Jesus and the extravagant spiritual wealth she's received in him.

Giving Says Something Eternal

Giving displays the glory of God and in this way material giving results in eternal treasure. What will last forever are not the things in this world, but the souls in this world and, significantly, the story our lives tell about the goodness and glory of God. Heaven is an eternal celebration of God—as we look through all that has happened here on earth and see how it has so perfectly revealed the magnificence of our Creator in his power, justice, mercy, love, and kindness (Rev. 15:4). Giving displays the glory of God—it's a statement that will last forever.

Every time you give, you're making a statement that God is better than anything else you could have done with that money. Sometimes giving requires just a little bit of faith. Other times, you're *incredibly* tempted to do something else with that money, and giving it away takes a lot of faith. Yet when giving requires faith, the statement you make about God's worthiness is all the more powerful, isn't it? Hebrews 11:6 says that "without faith it is impossible to please [God]." It's your faith that turns a financial transaction into something of eternal value.

Does your giving do this? Is it respectable in the eyes of this world? Or is it crazy and foolish from the world's perspective because you're risking everything on the promises of God? Risk everything on what God has promised! There's no safer place to be.

What If I Don't Want to Give?

Of course, sometimes we don't feel the joy of giving. What to do then? First, you could give with a grumpy spirit. That's the worst option. Giving in this way lies about God. Giving with a grumpy spirit communicates that God is a miserly master who demands your money even though there's a better way to use it.

Second, you could *spend* the money instead of giving it. This is better, but it's hardly the generosity that rescues our hearts from the empty promises of this world.

Or third, you can give. Not out of compulsion, but by faith, believing—despite what you feel—that it's good to give. And as giving becomes regular and habitual, your heart will follow your treasure, and your joy will abound.

It was this truth that first unlocked the joy of giving for me. When I got my first job, I gave to my church, but I'd have to say that my giving was more rote than cheerful. Then I began to see giving less as a financial transaction and more as an opportunity to show off the glory and goodness of my Savior. I discovered how fun it is to mock what this world values as I give it away. I learned the joy of taking real risks backed by the promises of God. And I began to understand the joy of being generous. That joy is yours to discover too!

Give for the sake of your heart. Give for the sake of your reward. And give to glorify God, which is what you were made to do. Now, glance back at your list of why you give on page 14. Would you change anything having read these three sections? Which reasons for giving that I've listed do you need to spend time thinking about?

But, of course, knowing *why* we should give is only a start. Where and how can we put these motivations into practice? That's the topic of the next two sections.

Where to Give? Your Church and God's Plans

Why Give to My Church?

So far in this booklet we've considered giving to God's purposes in general, but we haven't addressed the specific question on the front cover: Why should I give *to my church*?

As it turns out, the responsibility of Christians to give to their churches is all over the New Testament. Paul writes "The Lord commanded that those who proclaim the gospel should get their living by the gospel" (1 Cor. 9:14). What does that apply to if not those hearing that preaching? Similarly, in Galatians 6:6 he writes, "Let the one who is taught the word share all good things with the one who teaches." Are you taught the word in your church? Then this falls on you. Or consider 1 Timothy 5:17–18, a passage that instructs the church to pay its preacher. Where will that money come from if not the members of your church?

Clearly, God commands us to give to our churches. Of course, like with all of his commands, God's desire is that we give not because we have to but because we want to—because we really believe in his worth and promises. In that light, let me give you four reasons why, except in very unusual circumstances, most of your giving should go to your church.

Reason #1: The Local Church Teaches You

As we saw a moment ago, God places responsibility for paying teachers on those receiving the teaching—the church. The Bible teaching your church provides costs something. Are you investing in excellent teaching? What better investment could you make for your own soul?

Reason #2: The Local Church Will Prevail

Benjamin Franklin is famous for saying that nothing in this world is certain but death and taxes. Had he been a Christian, he might have mentioned a third: the local church. After all, no other institution has Jesus's promise of permanence: "I will build my church, and the gates of hell shall not prevail against it" (Matt. 16:18). It's like God whispering in your ear in 1890, "invest in the automobile" or in 1990 "invest in the Internet." In Matthew 16, Jesus is telling the apostles, "invest in the church; this one's gonna last." Jesus didn't promise that *every* church would last, but if you're going to pick something to invest in today that will someday yield eternal treasure, there's something especially attractive about the local church.

Reason #3: The Local Church Is Important

Ephesians 3:10 tells us that the local church is the centerpiece of God's grand plan to reveal the glory of his wisdom to all creatures under heaven. Acts 20:28 tells us that God bought the church "with his own blood." God cares deeply about your church! As a result, the local church is likely far more significant than most of us have understood. Many different Christian ministries are likely competing for your giving. Compared with them, your church may feel boring and un-inspiring. But we need to conform our ideas of "important" and "exciting" to the priorities of God's word in the Bible. When we do that, we will see great power and glory in the local church.

Reason #4: The Local Church Is Wise

In our individualistic society, we often think that no one else can tell us what to do with our money. But that's not a Christian attitude, is it? When you became a Christian, you submitted everything to the authority of the Lord Jesus Christ. And part of submitting to his authority is submission to the authority of your church (Heb. 13:17). When you give to your church, you are submitting the decision of how to invest your money for Jesus to your church and its leaders. The idea that you know better than your church is antithetical to biblical Christianity, be it with your morals or your money.

What If I Don't Trust My Church with My Money?

Perhaps as you read this booklet you're thinking *but you don't know my church! You don't know how (fill in the blank: inept, unspiritual, inefficient, greedy, etc.) they are!*

If this is your objection, I have a very simple reply: If you can't trust your church with your money, why on earth are you trusting it with your soul? Financial and spiritual realities go hand-in-hand. Remember Jesus's words: "Where your treasure is, there your heart will be also" (Matt. 6:21).

Of course, trusting your church doesn't mean that you agree with every way they spend every dime. Perhaps you wish they would spend a little less on staff and a little more on missions; perhaps you feel that the latest building renovation wasn't the wisest investment. I get that. For those situations, remember three things:

1) **No one is perfect.** Just like a stock portfolio is going to have some winners and losers, your church is going to spend money on things that in the final reckoning weren't the wisest spiritual investment. That's okay. The existence of a few unfortunate budget line items on the part of your church leadership in no way excuses you from the responsibility to give as you're able.

2) **Trust is required.** If you find your church to be trustworthy, then trust it. That means that sometimes you won't agree with what it does—but your posture should be one of trust. If the leaders have acted in such a way that you can no longer trust them, then you need to find a church where you can trust the congregation and its leaders.

3) **Discuss your concerns.** If there are ways
   your church spends its money that you don't
   agree with, find a leader in your church
   and speak with him about the matter.
   Don't make a big stink at a congregation-
   wide meeting, but serve the leaders of your
   church by humbly showing them where
   you think they might be mistaken.

So far we've answered the *why* and *where* questions of giving. That leaves one more important
question: *how*.

How to Give?

Paul's Instructions on How to Give

For many, the "how to give" question might
seem beside the point. "If I want to give, I just
open my wallet, right? How hard can it be?" But
we'll actually surrender a lot of joy if we don't
think more deeply about this question. Consider, for instance, 1 Corinthians 16:2:

> On the first day of every week, each of you
> is to put something aside and store it up,

as he may prosper, so that there will be no collecting when I come.

This verse has two implications for how we give:

Implication #1: Plan Your Giving. We often celebrate spontaneity as the height of spirituality, but that is not Paul's advice in this verse. Instead his advice suggests some level of planning: "put something aside" each week. Similarly, in 2 Corinthians 9:7, Paul writes "each one must give as he has decided in his heart." The Spirit is just as active in your life when you are planning your budget as when you are singing at church! Determining how much you should give should be a key component of creating a personal budget—and in fact, it should be a primary motivation for having a budget.

When you create a personal budget, you're essentially deciding how each dollar of income will go off to serve God's purposes. Some money will help you obey his command to provide for your family (1 Tim. 5:8). Some will help you obey the government as you pay your taxes (Rom. 13:7). And one of the best ways your money can serve God's purposes is as you plan to give it to his work in your church (Gal. 6:6). But of course, planning out your giving means that you must determine how much to give, which leads to the second implication of 1 Corinthians 16:2.

Implication #2: Give in Proportion to Your Income. Note Paul's exhortation for each to give "as he may prosper." In other words, if you make just a little bit of money, give just a little bit of money. If you make a large amount, give a large amount. Many Christians—and some entire denominations of churches—believe that Christian faithfulness requires that we give 10 percent of what we make (a tithe). After all, this is what God required his people to do in the Old Testament (Mal. 3:10). Other Christians argue that like animal sacrifices, the tithe was part of the Old Testament worship of God that has now been fulfilled in Christ (John 2:20–21).

I do not intend to settle this matter here. But I will argue that regardless of your view on the tithe, your responsibility does not end with 10 percent. Ten percent of what you make might be a great starting point for giving but in no way should we see it as all that God requires. Even in the Old Testament the people were expected to give beyond their tithe (Mal. 3:8). And in Christ, we have received what they could only dream of! Rather than seeing giving as an obligation, we should see giving as a privilege—and seek to give as much as seems wise given the different opportunities we have to serve Jesus in our lives.

Here are four questions to ask yourself about how much you're giving:

1) **Am I giving enough that it affects my heart?** If one reason for giving is to draw our hearts toward heaven, is my giving substantial enough to do that?

2) **Does anyone else know how much I give?** There are certainly ways we can talk about giving that are boastful that we should avoid (Matt. 6:3). But how strange would it be if we humbly sought counsel in other areas of struggle (like lust or fear) but never regarding money? After all, Jesus talked more about money than almost any other topic.

3) **What is the minimum proportion of my income that I hope to always give to my church?** As I said before, 10 percent is a great starting point—but in order to be faithful, many of us should be giving beyond that.

4) **Am I giving so much that it is damaging faithfulness in other parts of my life?** For example, I might give so much to my church that I am stingy toward my hungry neighbor. On the other hand, if the answer is "not by a long shot," then perhaps I need to be giving much more.

Do I Really Have To?

So often, our hearts complain about giving. We know it's not a good attitude, but it is what it is. As I often remind my congregation, if you have an attitude problem, it's because you have a gratitude problem. We give in order to show off the riches of what Christ has given to us (2 Cor. 8:8–9). We give to make much of our Savior (2 Cor. 9:11–12). We give because we love him (2 Cor. 9:7).

When we find we don't love him enough to give cheerfully, it means one of two things. First, it could be that we have forgotten the glory of the cross of Christ: how much we were forgiven, what it cost Christ, and how undeserving we were. Or, second, it could be that we have never been forgiven in the first place, that we are still lost in our sins. Because, as Jesus said, if we have been forgiven much, we will love much (Luke 7:47).

So take this matter of giving not as a reminder of your obligation but as a check on your heart. Do you love Jesus? Then give with all your heart, brother or sister! Grow in the grace of giving and anticipate the joy you will find as you do so (2 Cor. 8:7). On the other hand, as you finish this booklet are you finding that you don't love Jesus enough to give cheerfully? Then I have good news, friend: that can change! Confess this sin to God. Your hard-hearted giving has lied about his goodness and generosity. Confess this sin and believe that only Jesus's death on your behalf can take away the penalty of that sin. Confess, believe, and repent, choosing to follow him in all aspects of life. And talk to a Christian you trust about what you've been discovering about yourself.

God Loves a Cheerful Giver

In summary, we should conspire together in how we can use our money to proclaim the excellence of our great God and Savior, Jesus Christ. And that is an invitation to joy! Give to your church, and see your heart loosen its hold on the cheap "treasures" of this world. Give to your church, and look forward to the reward that awaits you above. Give to your church, and find the joy that comes from using even your money to show off the glory and wonder of Jesus. Give cheerfully, not because you have to but because you want to, because you trust that what God has for you is far better than anything your money could buy.

Other Questions

Below are some short answers to questions Christians frequently ask about giving.

1. Should I Give Online?

Some forms of online giving (e.g. setting up regular withdrawals from your bank account) facilitate the deliberate, planned approach to giving that Paul encourages in 1 Corinthians 16:2. But don't let that planned, automatic giving simply become "out of sight and out of mind." Other formats (e.g., giving by texting a dollar amount to a certain phone number) are often used to encourage giving in the heat of the moment, which is quite contrary to what Paul advocates in 1 Corinthians 16. Online giving removes giving from the weekly church service—but given that we have no clear examples of giving as part of corporate worship in the New Testament, many find this to be acceptable.

2. Should I Give to Causes in Addition to My Church?

Paul's instruction in Galatians 6:6, 1 Corinthians 9:14, and 1 Timothy 5:17 to support the teaching we receive suggests that giving to your church should be primary. At the same time, nothing in Scripture discourages giving to other ministries as well if you have the means and desire.

Let me offer a few guidelines for this extra giving. First, it should be above and beyond what you have decided to commit regularly to your church. Second, ask a pastor or another mature Christian you trust about a ministry you'd like to support since it does not have the benefit of being evaluated by the leaders of your congregation as part of the church budget. Finally, there is no reason why all of your giving as an individual should be to Christian organizations. But keep in mind that while non-Christians will also fund other worthy organizations, only Christians will fund the work of the gospel.

3. Should I Give If I Have Debt?

The short answer is that it depends. The most important guidance I can give you is don't make this decision alone; talk through your situation with another Christian you trust (Prov. 15:22). Here are a few principles to keep in mind:

- Christians are morally obligated to pay back their debts (Ps. 37:21).
- Debt is *always* a form of servitude (Prov. 22:7). There is no such thing as "good" and "bad" debt. But the degree to which that servitude constrains our ability to serve Christ varies

depending on our ability to meet the agreed-upon payments.

- Getting out of debt is *not* the goal of life; the goal of life is to serve Jesus Christ—and sometimes debt is a prudent way to do that (such as helping you purchase a home where you can be hospitable and provide for your family).

In general, if debt is a sustainable part of your budget, giving should also be a sustainable part of your budget. If you only have enough income to supply for your basic needs and pay your debts, you may be in the unfortunate position where giving would mean disobeying God's clear commands to pay your debts or care for your own needs (1 Thess. 4:12; 1 Tim. 5:8). In that case, I would encourage you to escape the situation by working with creditors to address the crushing load of your debt (Prov. 6:3), seeking extra income, reducing your expenses, and considering whether you need to redefine what really is a "need."

4. How Do I Balance Giving with Saving?

I remember a church member with a good salary who told me how he was living on nearly nothing, saving nothing, and giving a huge amount of money away. I loved his enthusiasm for the gospel! But I told him that I felt he was wrongly presuming on God by living his life this way. God's normal means of provision in the future is his provision in the present. To ignore that reality by giving away all of our surplus means ignoring his normal means of provision. That is not faith but presumption. Many people in this world have no surplus, and God will provide for their future needs. But if he has given you enough money to provide for your basic needs, give to your church, and have money left over, the Bible would encourage you to save some of it (Prov. 21:20; 1 Thess. 4:12).

How much should you save? That depends on many factors. If you don't know much about your future needs, you might pick an amount to give that seems substantial and proportional to your income and then save the rest. At some point in life, many people come to have a good sense of their future needs in which case you can start to budget your savings just like you budget your spending. Remember that many Christians mistakenly place their hope in their savings instead of in God; be aware of that temptation as you determine how much to save (Matt. 6:25–34).

5. How Do I Balance Giving with Spending?

Let's say you give an amount to your church that seems faithful, you have enough to provide for your basic needs, and you are saving what you need. Yet God has provided you with yet more money. Praise God! How much more do you give? You will struggle to answer that question well until you realize that there is one goal for all the money God has entrusted to you: to show off the glory of his name (1 Cor. 10:31). You show off his goodness by using money to enjoy good gifts (1 Tim. 6:17), by obeying his commands to provide for current and future needs (1 Thess. 4:12), and by giving. The question you must answer is whether your current budget is the *best* way to allocate your resources between all these opportunities to show off the goodness and glory of God.

6. How Do I Get Started Giving in a God-Glorifying Way?

Great question! Let me propose the following:

First, starting next paycheck, give 10 percent of it to your church.

Second, over the next few weeks, carve out some time to put together a budget if you don't have one (see an example on the next two pages). Try to articulate for *every* line item how that money is accomplishing God's purposes, and based on working through your budget, see if 10 percent is the right amount to be giving.

Third, sit down with a mature Christian friend to discuss your conclusions with them.

Fourth, repeat this once each year.

Sample Budget

*Examples of How Each Item
Can Bring Glory to God*

Income	$	Work exists to provide for your needs and to be generous with others (Eph. 4:28).
Taxes	$	Governments are to be obeyed unless this would be disobedient to Christ (Rom. 13:7).
Giving		Eph. 4:28
Church	$	We should give to support the teaching we receive (Gal. 6:6).
Missionary	$	Provide for missionaries "in a manner worthy of God" (3 John 6–8).

Mercy Ministry	$	We should provide for fellow Christians and then for others' needs (Gal. 6:10).
Housing		Housing helps provide for your family as 1 Timothy 5:8 instructs, helps us provide for our own needs (1 Thess. 4:12), and enables hospitality (Rom. 12:13).
Rent/ Mortgage	$	
Furnish-ings	$	
Repair	$	
Healthcare		
Doctor/ Insurance	$	Good health is part of how we make the most of the opportunities God gives (Eph. 5:16).
Gym	$	There is some value to physical training, though more to spiritual training (1 Tim. 4:8).
Telecom	$	Modern tools help you do what you do better, since you do it for Christ (Col. 3:23).
Transpor-tation	$	Transport enables you to provide for your needs and those of your family (2 Thess. 3:10).

Leisure		
Vacation	$	Proverbs reminds us of the wisdom of stopping periodically to rest (Prov. 23:4).
Meals Out	$	Use a dinner out to glory in God's goodness as you enjoy his gifts (1 Tim. 4:4).
Media	$	Non-sinful entertainment, received with thanks, honors the God who gave it (1 Tim. 6:17).
Personal		
Clothing	$	We honor God when we are content with our basic needs provided for (1 Tim. 6:8).
Groceries	$	Feeding your family and yourself is a basic command for every Christian (1 Tim. 5:8).
Home Supplies	$	Keeping a home allows you to be hospitable (Rom. 12:13).
Generosity		
Gifts	$	First Timothy 6:18 calls us to live in a way that is generous.

Other Generosity	$	Some opportunities for generosity happen without much notice (Luke 6:30–31).
Savings	$	God's normal means of provision in the future is our work today (2 Thess. 3:6–12).
Unallocated	$	Money without a job description puts us at risk of hoarding (James 5:1–3).

Notes

1. "Giving USA 2015 Press Release," The Giving Institute, 2015, accessed August 6, 2020, https://www.giving institute.org/page/GUSA2015Release.

2. "The Ultimate List of Charitable Giving Statistics for 2018," NP Source, accessed August 6, 2020, https://nonprofitssource.com/online-giving-statistics/.

3. Consider, for example, Paul's long section on giving in 2 Corinthians 8–9. He barely even mentions the need that motivates his request. And he bends over backward to emphasize that the Corinthians are not *obligated* to give (8:8).

4. Later on, we'll talk about how giving even though we don't feel like it—because we trust God—can still be the joyful, opportunity-driven giving that glorifies God.

5. For more on this, you might read Costi Hinn, *God, Greed, and the (Prosperity) Gospel* (Grand Rapids, MI: Zondervan, 2019). Costi Hinn is the nephew of famed "faith-healer" Benny Hinn and a former proponent of the "prosperity gospel."

6. John Piper, *Desiring God: Meditations of a Christian Hedonist*, rev. ed. (Colorado Springs, CO: Multnomah Books, 2011), 94.

Scripture Index

9Marks

Building Healthy Churches

9Marks exists to equip church leaders with a biblical vision and practical resources for displaying God's glory to the nations through healthy churches.

To that end, we want to see churches characterized by these nine marks of health:

1. Expositional Preaching
2. Gospel Doctrine
3. A Biblical Understanding of Conversion and Evangelism
4. Biblical Church Membership
5. Biblical Church Discipline
6. A Biblical Concern for Discipleship and Growth
7. Biblical Church Leadership
8. A Biblical Understanding of the Practice of Prayer
9. A Biblical Understanding and Practice of Missions

Find all our Crossway titles and other resources at 9Marks.org.